"Everybody should read this book!"

"Princess...or Pauper is an interesting and extremely fascinating read! I couldn't put it down. As I was reading it, I was visualizing and working through each area of the book in my mind and cannot wait to implement what I have learned. I think everybody should read this book!"

-DEBORAH MORGAN, CPA & AUTHOR OF
I've Got A Business, Now What?

"Amazing results!"

"Feng Shui may have been developed a long time ago, but the principles still apply incredibly well. This book is full of interesting and informative ideas—I picked up so many useful tips and, although I cannot implement them all at once, I have already seen amazing results!"

-JILL K. BASSETT, MARKETING WRITER, POET &
Busy Working Mother

"Why would you settle for less?"

"They used to say 'it takes a village.' Now more than ever, in these economic times, we all need help and support from others. But what about your home? You work hard to pay the rent or the mortgage. Isn't it time you look to your home to support you in your goals and bring prosperity to you? Make your home one of your biggest allies in your quest for success. Why would you settle for less? This book will show you how to not settle."

-LISA SCHOTT, AUTHOR OF
101 Ways to Cook Big Bear Lake Trout

Includes:

19 exercises to help you
on your way to wealth

Simple 3-Step Clutter Clearing Guide

Princess
...or Pauper?

What Your Feng Shui Reveals and How YOU Can Change It

Helen Arabanos

Princess…or Pauper?

What Your Feng Shui Reveals and How YOU Can Change It

2nd Book from the *Walls Do Talk* Series

Copyright © 2012 Helen Arabanos

All rights reserved, including the right to
reproduce this book or portions thereof
in any form whatsoever.

For more information:
Full Bloom Feng Shui

www.FullBloomFengShui.com

ISBN: 978-1480195233, 1480195235

First Edition published 2012

Edited by Jill K. Bassett

Printed in the United States of America

Other Titles by Helen Arabanos

HE'S INTO YOU...But Is His Home?

What a man's Feng Shui can reveal about him

Released June 2011

Athlete or Ailing?

Is your home's Feng Shui making you sick?

Available 2013

Princess
...or Pauper?

What Your Feng Shui Reveals and How YOU Can Change It

Helen Arabanos

In Loving Memory of Oliver

WINSTON CHURCHILL
"We shape our buildings; thereafter they shape us."

Table of Contents

History of Feng Shui and Wealth 1
What is Wealth? 5
    Exercise #1 8
Receiving 11
    Exercise #2 15
Your Clutter 19
    Exercise #3 24
Water Features 27
    Exercise #4 (Optional) 31
Stairs 33
    Exercise #5 (Optional) 36
Your Bedroom 39
    Exercise #6 43
Your Front Door 47
    Exercise #7 51
Your Entry/Foyer 53
    Exercise #8 58
Your Kitchen 65
    Exercise #9 69
Your Living Room 73
    Exercise #10 77
Your Dining Room 81

Exercise #11	86
Your Bathroom	**89**
Exercise #12	95
Your Closet	**97**
Exercise #13	100
Your Art	**103**
Exercise #14	107
Your Furniture & Home Accessories	**111**
Exercise #15 – Part I	113
Exercise #15 – Part II	115
The Palace Grounds	**119**
Exercise #16	122
Your Car	**125**
Exercise #17	129
Your Place of Work	**131**
Exercise #18	134
Your Purse & Wallet	**137**
Exercise #19	141
Appendix A: Clutter Clearing Guide	**I**
Appendix B: Recommended Reading	**XI**

History of Feng Shui and Wealth

Feng Shui was developed over 5,000 years ago in China. Its use was limited to the ruling class, and the Feng Shui practitioners were responsible for the entire building process.

They acted as realtor, choosing the location to build on. They acted as architect, designing the layout of the building. They acted as construction manager, overseeing the entire construction process to make sure the harmony of the landscape was not disrupted; this included telling the builders when they could start building and in which direction they could, or could not, work in a particular time period. They acted as building inspector, having final approval of the finished building.

The Feng Shui Masters were paid very well for their services. The ruling class believed it was so powerful that it gave them their edge over the commoners. They wanted to keep themselves elevated above the commoners and, therefore, only they were allowed to reap the benefits of Feng Shui.

Feng Shui practitioners could also be severely punished or put to death if they were caught advising the commoners. Luckily that is not the case today, and anyone can experience the benefits through the guidance of a trained Feng Shui practitioner. Consider this: just by your utilizing Feng Shui, you have already created a similarity between yourself and the wealthiest of rulers in history.

What is Wealth?

Everyone's definition of wealth may be different. For some it means having a lot of money. For others it means having a large family, or good health. And there are those for whom it means having food to eat or a bed to sleep in.

For this book, we will use wealth to refer to monetary wealth. That doesn't mean you can't also apply the concepts and ideas herein to other areas of your life for which you want abundance. You may need to do some modifications, however, and that is fine. You'll know when you are inspired to do so. Giving yourself the freedom to do that is in alignment with allowing yourself to receive.

To have wealth, you must first be clear on what that means to you. Know what you want, but don't get overly focused on how to get there. Yes, you need to have goals, ideas, action plans, etc. You may also think you know how to go about increasing your wealth. However, it's best to be open to its showing up in unexpected ways. If you get so focused on one path to wealth, you could actually be blocking other opportunities to receive wealth.

See Exercise #1 on the following page.

Exercise #1

Create your definition of wealth. What will you have? How would you spend your time? With whom would you spend your time? How would your life be different than it is now? How would it be the same as it is now?

Be sure to get a complete image of what your life would be like if you had the wealth you desire. This goes beyond just identifying a dollar amount you would like to have. Get clear on what your life would be like if you had that dollar amount.

Receiving

To be wealthy, you need to be able and willing to receive freely. Many people in this culture were raised to be selfless and thus are uncomfortable receiving. Childhood experiences vary, but often we were taught it's not polite to ask for what we want. Maybe you were told that nice girls don't ask for things, or something similar to that. Remember cutting the last brownie in half? You desperately wanted the bigger half but you did the "nice" thing and gave it away. Or you wanted the last cookie but didn't dare take it because it wouldn't be polite.

How are you at receiving compliments? This can be an indicator of how easily and freely you receive in general. If you have difficulty receiving a compliment, you may have difficulty receiving gifts, or wealth.

I once attended a very popular wealth building workshop. Early the first day we did an exercise about receiving. We walked around the room and complimented one another. Complete strangers, on the spur of the moment, came up with compliments for each other! We were instructed that our response to the compliment was to be a very simple "thank you."

For most, this exercise was a challenge. Many wanted to explain or refute the compliment. For example, if someone was complimented on the shirt they were wearing, their automatic reaction was something similar to the cliché "Oh, this old thing?" Or if they had been complimented on their hair, they wanted to say "Oh! It looks terrible today."

We did this exercise for maybe 10 minutes. It got easier for some, mainly because they knew it was a safe environment to accept and receive graciously.

How do you accept compliments? If you have a hard time accepting compliments it is likely that you have a difficult time receiving other things such as gifts, donations, rewards, abundance, and wealth by any definition.

Sometimes people who are really averse to receiving have a difficult time receiving even simple things. A simple "thank you" from someone for whom they have done a nice deed can be difficult for them; they dismiss it with the cliché "Oh, it was nothing."

Give up the concept of having to do your fair share. Consider that you already are doing that (and maybe more) and start enjoying receiving. Remember the thrill you got as a young child when you found a penny on the ground? There was no minimizing the gift, or dismissing it or leaving it on the ground and walking by. You picked it up and jumped for joy, telling whomever you were with, or the next person you saw, "Look what I found!" Recapture that joy of receiving, no matter how "small" the gift may seem.

Exercise #2

Practice receiving.

Practice receiving compliments, assistance, gifts, and smiles. Practice saying "thank you" graciously. That's it—just say "thank you" without any explanation, excuse, or invalidation.

For example, next time the bagger at the grocery store checkout asks if you want help to your car, answer affirmatively. Receive from someone help that you don't need, just because you can.

When someone compliments your clothing, accessories, hair or an action you did, just say "thank you." Don't qualify it or dispute it. If you just sang Karaoke, don't point out the words you messed up or the one sour note, or how nervous you were. Say "thanks!" You can even add something like, "I'm so proud of myself for getting up there and singing!"

Yes, complimenting yourself is okay. Do it in moderation and with modesty if you are doing it in front of other people. But what's stopping you from looking in the mirror and telling yourself that you look great? Or patting yourself on the back for the great job you did at work that day, even if no one else seemed to notice what you did?

Continued on the following page.

Exercise #2 Continued

You may want to journal about this experience. Make notes on what was hard about it, what caused you discomfort, which compliments or actions were the hardest to receive with a simple "thank you," and which acts of receiving may have caused guilt or other disempowering emotions. Include words to describe those emotions.

Notice any patterns: Do your words all have to do with a lack of deserving or guilt or perhaps a need to suffer? There is no right or wrong; it's just about becoming aware of what your feelings are with regard to receiving.

Your Clutter

A common term used in western Feng Shui, although not that common in traditional Feng Shui, is *clutter*. Clutter generally accumulates from one or two thought patterns: Fear and Scarcity. The concept of *scarcity* is often a *fear* of not having, rather than a reality of not having. Thus, clutter really accumulates from fear, and fear alone—fear of not having enough, or fear of not having a particular item that may be needed *at some point in the future.*

Do you live in scarcity? Do you keep things because you think you might need them someday? What do you think that is telling the universe? It's saying "Hey, Universe! I might need this someday and when that happens, I won't have the ability to obtain it so I'm going to hang onto it now, just in case!" What does that do? It tells the universe that you are willing to believe you won't have enough when you need it. Isn't that kind of like saying "stop giving to me" because I will hoard now just in case?

Isn't that the mentality that led to the bank runs during the great depression? How many of us have parents or grandparents who were raised during the depression? If that is true for you, chances are they have taught you to behave as if you were living during the depression. It's no surprise that with the current state of our economy, so many of us fall easily into that hoarding mentality: afraid to spend now because we may need it tomorrow or next month and may not have it.

It's a fine line between being responsible with our money and living in fear of not having enough. Look at the things you hang on to and ask yourself why you are hanging on to them. If it's not something you use on a regular basis (meaning at least once a year or more) or it's not something you love, then you are quite possibly keeping it for fear-based reasons.

The amount of available storage space you have access to can impact the choices you make. Do you over-fill the storage and/or living space that you have, thus creating clutter? What are the things you are keeping?

What if storage space is scarce? Do you seek additional storage space? Do you let it sit empty just in case you need to store something in the future? Think about that. It sounds absurd, but it is basically the same thing as hoarding objects for possible use at a later date.

If you've ever weighed a few extra pounds then you know that the additional weight made you uncomfortable and caused it to be harder for you to move around. Most likely your flexibility was impaired as well, along with your energy level. The excess weight causes a scarcity of energy.

The same is true with clutter around the home. It's harder to maneuver through your home; finding things in closets, drawers, or cabinets can be challenging, and you just don't feel well. Excess clutter creates scarcity of space. It also creates scarcity of peace-of-mind and scarcity of an inviting home.

There are two types of clutter: Active and Stagnant. Active clutter consists of the stacks, piles and projects that you are currently working with—the items you are interacting with on a frequent and regular basis. As long as you are interacting with something, it is a work-in-progress and does not drain energy. *As long as it remains active.* Active clutter does not drain Chi or life energy because it is moving.

When you begin to neglect a project, it becomes stagnant. Stagnant or inactive clutter is the second type of clutter. It includes those things that sit idle such as stacks of old magazines or newspapers, piles of unopened mail, and unused exercise equipment. Projects that were started months or years ago but have not been worked on since you can't remember when are a common form of stagnant clutter. Stagnant clutter drains energy.

Have you ever seen a wealthy home with clutter? If you were moving into your dream home, would you take your clutter with you?

Don't confuse clutter with being messy. Neat people have clutter, too! It is perhaps less noticeable because they are neat or well-organized. But that just means they can fit more unnecessary stuff into smaller spaces.

Remember, clutter is the items you don't need or use on a regular basis. Clutter drains Chi, valuable life energy, from you and your environment. At the back of this book is a guide you can follow to simplify the process of clearing your clutter. Here are a few basic tips to get you started right away.

1. Don't force yourself to do it all at once. Instead pick 3 things you know you want to release and get rid of them now.

2. Clearing clutter is a gradual and constant process. Just like you acquired your things gradually over time, releasing them can happen over time, and should happen continuously.

3. Keep a bag or box handy, so when you see something to release, you can place it in the box and it is then one step closer to being removed from your space.

4. Start with those things you are sure you want to eliminate. Don't challenge yourself to make decisions about items that you're not sure about. Remove the easy items first. The others will be easier to release after that.

5. Don't think about how to dispose of them yet; first decide to remove them. You can figure out how to dispose of them later.

Exercise #3

Begin to clear your clutter. Remove three things today that you know you are ready to release. Easy items to start with include clothes that no longer fit, items that are broken, things you no longer like, and items you no longer use frequently. Removing three or more items begins the shift in energy.

Keep that momentum going; use the Clutter Clearing Guide at the end of this book to continue on your clutter clearing process. Don't pressure yourself to do it all in one day; but if you get inspired, keep going!

Water Features

Any Feng Shui book about wealth and prosperity would not be complete if it didn't address water features – fountains, ponds, fish tanks, pools, etc. Water features are a commonly used tool in Feng Shui and are even more commonly misunderstood.

Myth: place a water feature near your front door and wealth will enter your home.

Think of water features as medication. Just as everyone doesn't need the same type of medication, every home does not need a water feature in the same location. Randomly placing a water feature is like randomly taking a medication to see if it makes you feel better.

Water features activate energy, very specific types of energy. Some energy in Feng Shui "likes" activity, other energy "likes" and responds to stillness. Some energy is favorable; some is not-so-favorable. Placing a water feature in an area with one of these not-so-favorable energies that likes activity will empower it and make it stronger. This is definitely not something you want to do. It could inadvertently cause arguments, health issues, or other adverse experiences.

If you have not had your home analyzed by a Feng Shui professional, you'd be taking a risk placing a water feature without their guidance. Would you take a prescription medication without first consulting a physician? Then why would you give your home medication without consulting a *house doctor*?

In Feng Shui, water features are placed very specifically to activate what is called the *Noble Water Star*. Every 20 years, and sometimes when major work is done on the home, the location of this *Noble Water* Star changes.

The water feature is best left running 24/7, provided it is in the proper location. Without the advice of a professional, it's best to avoid using water features. If you insist on using one, it's best to run it only occasionally, and for only short periods of time.

If you are feeling lucky, or brave, turn the water feature on and be aware of any changes you experience. Watch for changes in your health, or your relationships, or your money, or stress. If the changes you experience are not favorable, then you know you don't have the water feature in the correct location. Feeling overwhelmed or irritated by the sound is a common indicator of a fountain misplaced.

Does every home need a water feature? No. There are some homes whose *Noble Water Star* is "locked" in the center and, therefore, has no place to put the water feature. Well, that's not exactly true. If you know where the Emperor Star is located, you can place a water feature there—*IF,* and only *IF,* it can be seen from the center.

I realize much of this chapter and the terms used are complicated and confusing and that I haven't explained them. Explaining them is far too complex for the scope of this book. My point is to show how complicated the placement of a water feature can be and why placing one randomly and letting it run is not recommended.

Also be aware that sometimes when things are feeling stagnant, placing a water feature, even in the wrong place, may seem to improve things for you. Be careful, as this is part of the "charm of the devil," lulling you into thinking it's helping you, and when you forget about it, the real energy rears its ugly head. By then you may be caught up in the drama you are experiencing in life. You've likely long forgotten about the water feature randomly placed, although simply turning it off may very likely alleviate the issues you are experiencing.

So in case I haven't made it clear, be very cautious about placing a water feature in or around your home unless you are following the advice of a trained Feng Shui professional. Make sure they are trained in traditional Flying Star Feng Shui. I'm not saying that other methods aren't valid; they are, but I'm simply saying that I wouldn't use a water feature with other methods as the effects can be very unpredictable.

> **Exercise #4 (Optional)**
>
> If you have any water features in your home or yard, turn them off for a few days--all of them. Then turn one on for a few days. Notice what happens in the few days that it's on. Do you feel more optimistic and productive? Do you feel irritable? Do you feel crazed or "too" busy?
>
> Try this for each of your water features, one at a time. Notice which ones make you feel good and/or bring in positive events or opportunities.
>
> Notice which ones make you feel low energy, or aggravated, or irritable. Notice which ones create drama, chaos, or overwhelm you in your life.
>
> Based on your feelings and experiences, you'll know which one(s) you may want to turn off permanently and which ones you may be willing to let run occasionally.

Stairs

Ahh... the stairs going to the front door. Is this really such a huge problem? It can be, only in very specific circumstances.

The belief is that if the stairs lead to your front door then your wealth will fall out the door. In actuality, the Chi is likely to rush out your door because it has gained momentum coming down the stairs (like tumbling down a hill) and it's possible that your wealth could get caught up in the current and go out the door along with your Chi.

Either way, Chi, with or without wealth, is not something you want rushing out your door. The door is considered the mouth of chi and we want favorable life energy, Sheng Chi, to enter the door, not exit the door.

To be clear, it's not an issue of being able to *see* the stairs from the door; it's an issue of the stairs being directly in front of the door. Specifically, if you walk in the front door and take a couple of steps forward, are you at the foot of the stairs, looking up at the entire staircase?

If you have to turn to the right or left, you're not likely to lose Chi from this. If you have to go around a wall, or a piece of furniture, to get from the stairs to the front door, your energy is not likely to be rushing out of it.

If the stairs are set back from the door, it should not be a problem. Simply place something between the door and the stairs such as a chair, a table, a plant or a statue. If you have to walk around it, then Chi has to move around it also. This slows down the movement *and* redirects it, thus preventing it from tumbling out your front door.

See Exercise #5 on the following page.

Exercise #5 (Optional)

Do you have stairs inside your home or outside leading toward your home? If so, walk up or down the stairs and walk a straight path. What is the first thing you encounter? Is it a door, a table, or a piece of furniture? Perhaps it's something that doesn't belong there, like a pair of shoes or a tote bag that wasn't put away?

If you walk directly from the stairs to your front door, then there is a good chance your Chi, and possibly your wealth, may be escaping. If this is the case, place an object between the stairs and the door to help detour the Chi and slow down the escape of wealth.

If you encounter anything but the door, this is great! You've already done a good job of creating a detour. If the item you encounter doesn't belong there, replace it with something that can stay there such as a statue or plant, a chair or a table. Even a rug can help slow and detour Chi, as long as it doesn't become a potential hazard for tripping.

Now that we've covered some of the basics, keep them in mind while we take a look at the various rooms and areas of your home.

Your Bedroom

Traditionally the bedroom is one of the three most important areas in a home. For many people, the majority of their at-home time is spent in the bedroom. Therefore, its energy is likely to have the largest impact on the occupants. The more time you spend in an area, the more it will impact you.

Think back to childhood when your parents told you that people judge you by the friends you associate with. It's a similar concept in Feng Shui. People's experience with you is based on the Feng Shui energy of your home and, specifically, the energy in the area of your home in which you spend the most time.

When I was a little girl, I longed to have a canopy bed. I didn't get one until well into adulthood. The first night I slept in it felt very decadent. When I woke up in the morning and saw the pillars draped with sheer fabric all around me, I immediately felt like a princess. I think I even involuntarily said out loud "I feel like a princess!"

Whether or not a canopy bed is your preference, your bedroom should *and can* make you feel like a princess. In so many homes that I see, the bedroom is the neglected room. It's a "private" room and, therefore, many do not bother to decorate it.

I see it in homes that have been professionally done by an interior decorator: the entire home is beautiful, except for the bedroom(s). The occupants ran out of money, or time, or just got tired of the activity involved to decorate the space. But regardless of the reason, the bedroom said "pauper," while the rest of the home said "princess."

Think about it--rather than enjoying long hours in the beautifully decorated areas of their home, people are likely to spend a few hours at the end of the day in these spaces and then retreat to the *pauperesque* bedroom for 7 or 8 hours, thus reinforcing the pauper mentality.

This has an underlying message of not being worthy or deserving. Only the rooms that other people see are tended to with care. The room you likely spend most of your time in is the least cared for. This is *not* the message you want to espouse.

Start with your bedroom. Even if you work from home, as I do, your bedroom is important. It is that retreat of luxury you go to at the end of your long day. It is the place you start each morning, feeling pampered and spoiled before you go out into the world. Make it luxurious, indulgent and inviting.

Remembering the guiding tenet that bedrooms are *for sleeping and romance only* can help you get your room fit for a princess.

> **Exercise #6**
>
> What's in Your Room? Look around your bedroom and make note of everything you see in plain site that is not related to either sleeping or romance. To help you, here are some of the things I commonly see in bedrooms that ideal:
>
> Desk, computer, television, multiple bookcases, athletic/sporting/exercise equipment (this includes your gym bag and ski poles), pet beds and toys (in excess), crafting/jewelry making supplies, art supplies, and family photos of others than you and your Prince Charming.

What did you see when you looked around? Are there clothes on the floor? Are they dirty or clean? Are the drawers open? Is the bed made? What is covering your bed? Is it something that makes you feel good, or does it depress you or generate some feeling in between?

Your bedroom should invite wealth and appear wealthy. Looking "busy" is one thing. You don't need to keep your room completely organized every moment. We all have times when we are rushed and don't put the clean (or dirty) clothes away. That's fine, as long as they get put away another time in the near future. After all, you do live in this space, and most of us don't have someone following after us to clean up...maybe not yet anyway!

Think of a luxury hotel. What makes you feel so spoiled when you are there? Often it's the fact that someone cleans your room and you come back to a bed that is made, clothes that are hung, and no towels on the floor. Well, consider taking the two minutes required to make your bed or to pick up your clothes, so when you return later you will have that same luxurious feeling.

Do you have pets, or children? Are their toys scattered around your bedroom? I'm saying this facetiously: how do your pets, children or their toys aid you in sleep or romance? Are your clothes, gym bag, or other items lying around on the floor? All those things can make for a hectic room and can impair sleep. A princess needs her rest, for health and beauty!

In case you haven't read my previous book, I want to address the concept of the *everything room*™. This is a concept I identified based on the many bedrooms I've seen in my practice.

When we were young, for many of us, our bedroom was our *everything room*™. We slept, studied, played, and entertained our friends there. For some it was even a place of punishment/banishment when we were naughty.

As adults, many people hang on to this concept and continue to have their bedroom be their *everything room*™. It may be due to lack of space (there's that scarcity thought pattern again), but often it is just out of habit and, for whatever reason, they haven't left the concept behind.

If your room is still your *everything room*™, take some time to begin to change that. If you hadn't thought about it before, and it's just been a pattern of habit, here is your opportunity to change that. What can you move out of your bedroom right now, to another place in your home?

If your bedroom is your *everything room*™ due to lack of space, consider this: How often do you have other people over to your home? So often I see that people rarely have guests over and yet they are more concerned about the public spaces of their home than their bedroom, where they spend most of their time. There could be a psychological cause for this, and there is definitely an impact.

You're treating those occasional guests as royalty and treating yourself as a pauper, day-in and day-out. Begin to shift this, and you'll begin to see a shift in your lifestyle.

For many, the bedroom is the hardest room to address. It's personal and private; it holds our secrets and our fears. Don't condemn yourself to do it. Give yourself time and do it gradually. Start on it now, and continue working on it as you read the other chapters of this book. By the time you finish the book, your bedroom may be fit for a princess. Or maybe it won't be, but it will definitely be more ready for the royals than it is now!

Your Front Door

We all know how important a first impression is. It can often make or break the way things go. It's no surprise that the first impression of your home, the front door, is considered to be another one of the three most important areas of a home in Feng Shui.

The front door is sometimes referred to as the *Mouth of Chi* – that place where Chi, life energy or life force, enters a space. If a person has difficulty finding, or getting to, your front door, then it's likely that wealth won't be able to find you either. Have you ever seen a palace or a mansion, or even a modest yet elegant home, for which the path to the front door was not clearly marked? It may not have been lined with guards, but chances are it was clearly marked.

Make sure the path is clear and well kept. No overhanging branches to duck under or overgrown foliage to step over or trip on. Is it swept and manicured? Is it free from clutter? If you have potted plants lining the path, are they next to the path or are they taking up space on it, making it difficult for people to traverse the path?

Keep walkways clear for people, Chi energy, and wealth to flow to you.

The Mouth of Chi is used to refer to the point where energy enters. So if you often use an entrance other than your front door, such as a garage or side entrance, be sure this is well maintained also.

Just as food enters your mouth, energy enters a home through an opening, most often the front door. But more and more these days, it is the garage door that is most used.

This opening should be clear and easily accessible for people and for Chi.

Lights and other markings, such as statues, paths, and plants, can help to draw people and Chi toward your front door with ease.

Consider placing a big "Welcome" sign or mat at your front door as a symbol that you are inviting prosperity into your home. Each time you see it, you will be reminded that wealth is welcome to come through your door with you.

Exercise #7

Go outside, to the street or driveway--wherever your guests would start their approach to your home. Look at it as if you've never been there before. Walk the path; notice and observe.

Is the path easy to travel or are there obstacles in your way? Is the location of the door clear, or do you have to ponder where the entrance is? Once you find it, is it welcoming and inviting? Is there any doubt that you are an expected and *wanted* guest?

Make any adjustments needed to make sure the guest's walk to your door is easy, pleasant, and welcoming.

If you were anticipating the arrival of a guest who was bringing you $1,000,000, would you do anything different to the path to your door? Would you add a larger sign with your house or apartment number? Would you add a light, a welcome mat, a plant, a statue, or a bench? Would you trim plants and trees, or perhaps plant some flowers?

Make a list of any changes you would like to make. Do as many as you can, as quickly as you can. Keep the list so that you can make any remaining changes as you are able to.

Your Entry/Foyer

Continuing on, let's look at the foyer or entry of your home. Traditionally in the Chinese culture, people would place their most prized artwork in their entry. The entry is the place that welcomes visitors and guests and also sends them safely on their way. They may pause here to remove shoes or coats, and thus it should be a place that shows respect and is worthy of praise.

If you have to step over or maneuver around obstacles to enter, then wealth and opportunities may have a difficult time finding you. Why not make it easy for wealth to enter your home?

You may have excuses, valid or not, such as "I travel a lot for work," "I'd rather do other things with my time than clean," "I need a bigger place," "I just got home," "I had to walk my dog," "I didn't have time to put my things away," or any other explanation for the items that have taken up residency in the entry of your home.

This may be true on occasion, but if it is the norm for you, consider that the excuses you make for not cleaning may give an indication of what is coming between you and the wealth you say you want. Make room for wealth to easily maneuver into your home.

Granted, a wealthy person would most likely pay someone to clean their home for them. If you don't have the time to do it yourself and don't have the money to pay someone else, try paying yourself to do it. Find a way to reward yourself for keeping your front entry free from clutter. There's a good chance that this will actually lead to your having the wealth to pay someone else, if that is what you'd like.

You've probably seen older movies in which butlers open the door for guests and show them into the drawing room. That speaks wealth. In Feng Shui, we refer to the first thing seen when entering a space as the **Greeter.** This can be a bench, a plant, a statue, a table, a lovely painting – anything that draws the eye and draws someone into the home with a welcoming feel. It can also draw wealth and opportunities into your home.

What is the first thing you currently notice when you walk in your door? Are you bombarded with many items or does one item stand out? Don't dismiss it; take special note of it. That first item, your greeter, is sending you a loud and clear message about your life, your view, and what you think of yourself.

You don't need to get too caught up in details and analyzing; just note if your greeter gives off a positive, neutral or perhaps negative vibe. Do you feel good when you see it? Does it bring you down? Do you dismiss it and move on to the next item, whether it is good or bad? These are the things to be aware of.

Are you greeted by several pairs of shoes? Shopping bags? School books or work you brought home from the office? A baseball bat or other sports equipment? What does that greeter tell you or make you think of? Does it make you feel wealthy or poor? The answer will tell you if you need to find a new greeter or not.

Does your greeter invite you in or block your path? Does it make you want to stop right where you are, or does it invite you to step forward and approach it or move further into the home? You want your greeter to invite you in, not stop you in your tracks. If you are invited in, wealth will also be invited in.

Imagine you are entering Buckingham Palace, Trump Towers, or the home of Oprah. What would you think if their entry looked and felt like yours? Would you question if you were in the right place? Would you say "Yes! I want to be here!" or "No! Get me out of here!"?

What impression would you have of the person who lives there? What did you notice? Did you like what you saw? Do you want to spend time with this person and get to know them better? Is it what you want people to think about you?

Does it represent the type of wealth you want in your life? Think about the types of opportunities you wish you had. If you had the chance to choose, strictly based on the front entry of a person's home, would you give those opportunities to someone whose entry looks like yours? Why or why not?

See Exercise #8 on the following page.

Exercise #8

Take a moment and think about the impression your entry would give to someone who doesn't know you. Someone who makes a judgment or decision about you based solely on the impression they get when they walk through your front door. After all, people often judge a book by its cover.

If you aren't sure, set this book down, go out your door, close the door, and walk a distance away. Then walk toward your door, open the door, and walk in. Observe as if you don't know the homeowner and have never been to this home before.

What do you notice first? What is your reaction to it? What assumption do you make of the person living in this home?

Is that the impression you want to give to visitors? Make a list of any ideas you have to wealth-up your entry.

When I first started consulting, I used to ask people how to get to their home. In a short time, I learned it was better not to ask. Since most people use a GPS or internet mapping service, people don't give directions much anymore. However, if there is something unique or a way to make it easier for your visitors to find you, tell them this ahead of time. By not asking for this information, I would get an indication of how inviting and welcoming they are. I could answer the question: Did they give me the bits of information needed to find them, especially if my GPS wasn't quite right, or did they let me fend for myself?

What does this have to do with attracting wealth? It's about energy. Wealth is energy. It finds you, just like visitors to your home, based upon the energy you transmit.

One client informed me that most of the electronic mapping systems gave the wrong directions, telling drivers to turn right onto her street when they should actually turn left. She made sure to tell me this when I was coming to her home for the first time. She is clearly someone who is welcoming visitors *and wealth* to come through her front door. This woman wants to make sure that she is found with ease. She cleared up any confusion. She sent a clear message to me, as an arriving guest, and to the universe.

Another client's home had a path that split into a Y, each arm leading to a different door. I went back and forth, not knowing which door I was being asked to enter. I chose the one that was closer and seemed to have clearer access. I chose the wrong one and found myself entering the home through a bedroom. I gave the client suggestions on how to differentiate and make the path to the front door clear and mystery free.

You can be creative when directing the flow of visitors to your home. In my previous home, after the foyer, there were two hallways--one to the left and one to the right. Both were carpeted, while the entry floor had a hard surface. The path to the left went to the living room, dining room and kitchen; the path to the right led to the bedrooms and bathrooms. People were always confused as to which way to go. The change in flooring created a stop sign of sorts. Guests would stop, look both ways, and then ask "which way do I go?" I retiled the floor of the entry and the hall to the public rooms with matching tile, and left the hall to the private rooms carpeted. This completely eliminated the confusion.

The hall to the bedrooms now had a different flooring. This created a sign of sorts that said "do not enter." Visitors stayed on the path of tile – acting as a "yellow brick road" that they just followed without any hesitation or thought required.

Before the change, there was confusion. After the change, there was no question. No words needed to be spoken; visitors automatically stayed on the matching tile floor that lead directly to the living room. Another option would have been to hang curtains or some other divider at the entry of the hallway to the private rooms. I chose the tile so that I didn't block Chi, and wealth, from flowing freely throughout my home.

This is just an example of the creativity and subtlety you can use to direct the flow of people and Chi energy in your home. Depending upon the architectural design, this may or may not be an issue in your home. If you aren't sure, try to recall your experience the first time you walked into your home. Was it clear which direction to go after entering? Did the flow feel natural to you? If so, great! If not, think about what you can do to create a smooth flow from entry to public rooms.

Many homes I go to place plants near the door. Yes, this makes a home warm and inviting, giving it a comfortable, lived-in feel. But be sure the plants don't overpower the door by having too many or too large plants. Potted plants can be trimmed back just like trees and shrubs. A well groomed plant is much more inviting than a plant growing wild.

Plants with pointed or spikey leaves are not friendly and inviting. Just the opposite; they can send a message of "stay away" by appearing subconsciously as a sword yielding guard whom one has to "get past" to enter the dwelling. Instead, choose plants with round, softer leaves near your door.

While on the subject of plants with respect to wealth and Feng Shui, we need to talk about **Money Trees**. Money trees are essentially a living, growing object representative of your money growing. Often I've heard people refer to Bamboo plants as money trees. Bamboo is really more representative of longevity than money. However, since most people want longevity of wealth, I can see how this could work as a money tree.

Some people use Jade plants. Again, jade plants tend to be easy care and long living. They have the additional benefit of rounded leaves, almost coin like in shape. This is really the key to choosing a money plant. Choose a plant that is lush, well-maintained, and has abundant round leaves that can be representative of coins.

Remember that when Feng Shui was developed thousands of years ago, money existed only in the form of coins. There were no dollar bills, no credit cards, no debit cards, and no PayPal accounts. Coins or gem stones (again, round in shape) were the standard form of money. Thus, the money tree should appear to be growing coins.

If it will help you to stay present to growing money, you could consider hanging some lucky Chinese coins, or other coins, on your money tree. This is not necessary nor a magical good luck charm; it's just a visual aid to help you keep the thought of money growing in your mind.

One woman I worked with recently had a medium-sized plant with spikey leaves next to her front door. We discussed the impact of this, and she immediately swapped it for a smaller mint plant that was elsewhere on her front porch. Wow! What a difference. We both made audible sighs. It really created a much more open, inviting and relaxed feeling at her front door.

Remember, "like attracts like," so if you want to attract wealth, you need to create a *like* space to attract it.

Allowing Chi to flow freely toward you will allow opportunities to find you easily. Opportunities lead to wealth. Block your front door, block your wealth.

Your Kitchen

As previously mentioned, traditionally in Feng Shui there are three important rooms or areas of the home. The kitchen, or more specifically the stove, is the third location of importance.

Why the stove? In part because when Feng Shui was developed thousands of years ago, people cooked on open fires outdoors. Only the extremely wealthy had any means to cook indoors; therefore, the mere presence of a stove implied wealth.

Look at the condition of your stove. You can look at your other appliances as well, but we will focus on the stove here. Is it clean? Does it work? Do all burners work or just some of them? Do you use all the burners or do you use only one or maybe two of them?

You may want to think of the burners as bank accounts. If you have several bank accounts, you are likely to pay attention to each of them. In the same way, occasionally you'll want to use each burner. That doesn't mean you have to use each burner all the time. But when you can, when it's convenient, think about using that small back burner from time to time.

Additionally, the stove is where you prepare the nourishment for your body. So it is something that should be treated with honor and respect for what it provides for you. Keeping a stove clean and in good working order is a simple way to show honor and respect to your stove, your body, and what you put into your body for nourishment.

This doesn't mean you have to go out and buy the newest, largest or most expensive stove. Many old stoves have such wonderful charm. Honor and respect what you have, and it will honor and respect you.

There are some in the Feng Shui industry who believe that, when moving into a new home, it is beneficial to cook something as soon as possible. Yes, moving day can be difficult, but it doesn't have to be an elaborate meal. Put a tea kettle on the stove, or warm up a can of soup; anything simple and nourishing or comforting is fine.

This custom is said to bring health, happiness and prosperity to the home. I can't say that I have any proof of this; however, it certainly can't hurt! Besides, it's a nice way to celebrate your first day in your new home.

What about dishes and small appliances? Quality, not quantity, especially if you have a smaller kitchen, is more supportive of wealth and helps you keep clutter to a minimum. Do you need 12 place settings of dishes, or will four suffice for most of your needs? If you can get by with four, perhaps you can obtain better quality.

I knew a woman who was very proud of her engagement ring. It was a small diamond by many people's standards, but the quality was spectacular! When she and her then husband-to-be went shopping for her ring, they agreed that quality was more important to them than quantity. This can be a good rule-of-thumb to follow in your kitchen as well.

Would you feel more wealthy eating off plastic plates (of which you have 12), or china plates (of which you have 4)? Maybe you would prefer something in between. That's fine. The point is, if your plates are old or cracked or chipped, or the pattern is warn or outdated, does that make you feel good when you set the table and sit down for a meal? Does it make you feel wealthy or poor? Would you enjoy that meal more on a nicer plate?

Exercise #9

Part I

Get your stove clean and in working order.

Part II

Your dishes may reflect the level of worthiness that you give to yourself. If Oprah, the Donald, or the Queen of England were coming to your home for a meal (or for tea or cocktails), would you feel confident serving them with your current dishes? If so, great! You are treating yourself like royalty, which is one of the best ways to reach that status!

If you wouldn't feel comfortable serving those guests with your current dishware, ask yourself where the cut-off point is. This means, do you serve yourself on those dishes? Do you serve your family on them? Friends? All friends or just some? Which ones? Would you serve your boss, a prospective date or potential in-laws? How about the governor of your state?

Notice where your cut-off point is. That is a reflection of the worthiness you give yourself. Are you as worthy as your neighbor? As the governor? Pay attention to this and start looking at how you can begin to shift the paradigm.

This doesn't mean that you have to eat off fine china for each and every meal. It does mean that you should give yourself the luxury of having at least a few dishes that make you feel grand, and allow yourself to use them from time to time—just because. You can use them to celebrate the end of a long work week, or to cheer yourself up when you are feeling down. Pamper yourself and the world will also find ways to pamper you.

Although we already addressed clutter in an earlier chapter, it is worth revisiting here while we talk about the kitchen. The kitchen is often a common place to accumulate clutter. One of the easiest and quickest ways to drain wealth is with clutter. As you've learned, there is nothing about clutter that says wealth. Clutter usually indicates exactly the opposite – a fear of scarcity or having a lack of something.

Whether it's your junk mail piled up on a table or counter top, or your dirty dishes in the sink, there is nothing about clutter that says "abundance". Even if your excuse is that you are busy working. Being busy is an indication of lack, or scarcity, of time. Is that part of your wealth vision? For most, the vision of wealth includes having enough time to enjoy the things they love to do.

Kitchens are often the gathering place in the home—the hub. People move to and from the hub on their journey to either another room or a location outside of the home. By the nature of the amount of activity in the hub, it is likely that there will be more of a mess—more items moving around or being placed on the surfaces or in the drawers. Don't let that be an excuse for clutter.

Go back to the previous references made to Donald Trump, Oprah, or your own wealth idol. Do you think they live with clutter in their kitchen? Yes, they have the means to pay, and likely do pay, someone to keep their dishes clean, their countertops clear, and their mail sorted as it arrives. But the point is that they likely don't live with clutter.

Just because you may not have the luxury of a housekeeper…yet…doesn't mean you should allow clutter to gather. Saying things like, "I'll do the dishes when I have time" or "when I can afford to pay someone to clean, I will have a clutter-free kitchen" puts your wealth further off in your future.

It would be like saying "I'll wear make-up/style my hair/dress nice/lose weight after I have a boyfriend." That sounds pretty silly, right? Those are the things women do to attract a man. We consider looking good and feeling good about how we look as necessities to finding a man.

Why would you think of wealth any differently? Does clutter attract wealth? Do dirty dishes attract wealth? Would someone with a fabulous wealth-creating opportunity be inspired to share that opportunity with you if they saw your kitchen right now?

Not only does clutter drain Chi and stave off wealth, it also brings most people's mood down. It can be depressing. Depressed people are less productive and less likely to reach their goals, wealth or otherwise.

Your Living Room

The Living Room...the name says it all - Living. It is often the most lived-in room of the house. And, we've all heard the term "lived-in" used to describe a home that may be somewhat messy or worn.

Is your living room lived in, or do you spend most of your time in another part of the home, "saving" the living room for when you have guests? I had a friend in my 20's who would host amazing parties at his parent's home in Beverly Hills...when his mom was out of town.

The living room was clearly off-limits by way of yellow *caution* tape across the doorway. Why? Because the living room contained expensive furniture, antiques, and other valuable accessories reserved for mature guests, which we were not. Keep in mind the rest of the home was quite lovely and would not have been described as "lived in," but it was space that young party-goers could be trusted to enter. Of course, the day following the party was the after-party – we all came back to clean up.

Is your home lived in, or does it have the feel of caution tape everywhere? Maybe there are areas of each. That is fine. Which of these areas do you spend the most time in? Do you allow yourself to enjoy the caution tape areas or do you banish yourself from that kingdom to dwell only in the lived in areas?

If the latter, think about the subliminal message this is sending you. It could be a message of unworthiness. Those areas are for only specific people, not you. You and you alone are not allowed to enjoy the finer areas of your home. Then why have those areas? Is your home for you or for someone else? This type of message is likely the case if the areas where you do spend time are old, worn, dirty or otherwise unappealing.

In the example I gave previously about my friend's parents' home, keep in mind that the rest of their home was also quite lovely. It was not "lived in" but was still a beautiful space to be in. I can't tell you if the family enjoyed the living room without guests or if they, too, were banished from it. But given the condition and décor of the rest of the home, it was still a self-honoring place to spend time.

So remember, it's fine to have areas that aren't used on a daily basis as long as you:

    a) Have the rest of your space set up in a way that is pleasant, appealing, and lovely.

OR

    b) "Allow" yourself to use them whether or not you have guests. If you aren't able to enjoy these spaces, what is the point? If you aren't worthy of them, what else do you believe you are not worthy of?

If you have small children, teenagers, or pets, that may impact the condition of your home. Just be sure you are living, and can afford to live, the way you choose rather than letting the children or pets dictate how you live.

I've heard many people explain their living conditions by telling me they have children or dogs. Yes, having children or pets to keep up with, and clean up after, is more work than living by yourself or with only working adults in the household. However, not every home with children or pets looks as lived in as others. Which end of the spectrum is your home?

I'm not saying there is anything wrong with a lived-in looking home. However, if you are at all embarrassed by it or feel the need to explain it, then it is likely not at the standard you would like.

Find a balance. It should be a space where you can relax and enjoy, and yet it should be a favorable reflection of you. It should be a place of respect for the occupants, one that you are proud of or at least comfortable with people seeing.

Related to what we've been discussing, but on a smaller scale, are the items with which you choose to surround yourself.

Exercise #10

Take an inventory of your living room or family room. Make note of those things you would keep if you were wealthy and living in your dream home. Also make note of the things you would definitely not take with you to your dream home.

Be aware that there may be some neutral items for you – those things that you don't feel strongly one way or another about taking with you or not. You can make lists, one for the "keep" items, one for the "release" items, and one for the neutrals. Or you may prefer to use colored stickers or post-it-notes for each category.

Continued on the following page.

Exercise #10 (Continued)

You don't have to clear everything out, but be aware of the number and types of items you have that you wouldn't be willing to take with you to your dream home. Are they things from family or friends? Are they things you use? Have you just gotten used to having those things around? Why wouldn't you take them with you? Are there any that you can freely, easily and comfortably release now?

Do the things you'd like to release outnumber the items you would take with you and, if so, by how much? It's okay to have some items you don't love, or even like, but your space and you will benefit if the number of things you would take with you to your dream home is greater than the number of things you'd leave behind. Start working in that direction.

It's okay if you don't feel you can release any of the items right now. The point is to become more aware of what you have surrounded yourself with.

You may notice over the next several days, weeks or months that these things start to irritate you and you may feel compelled to remove one or more of them. That's okay. In fact, it's great if you do – you will be releasing the pauper in you and making room for the Princess! But don't force it or you could slip back. Allow the progression and release to happen organically. When it does, it will feel right. Of course, a little nudging can't hurt.

Your Dining Room

Dining rooms often have a number of purposes other than dining, except during holidays. But whatever your dining room's everyday purpose is, it can still be part of the team supporting your wealth goals.

I have seen neglected or forgotten dining rooms. I have seen dining rooms that are offices, or play rooms, or storage areas. I have even seen a dining room with multiple beds for the owner's drinking buddies to crash on when they'd drank too much to drive. Whatever your dining room has been converted into, keep your wealth goals present.

Let's go through the examples I've listed. Suppose your dining room is a "crash pad" for your drinking buddies. How do you make that support your wealth goals? It's easy; make sure those spare beds have wealthy looking bedding covering them. Throw pillows or bedspreads with gold trim or of rich,, jewel-toned colors, for example, can lift the wealth Chi of this room.

You don't have to spend a lot to make it look like you did. Just make the bed accessories match or at least coordinate them, and the room will instantly look more wealth conscious than if the beds were covered with mismatched or left-over bedding.

If your dining room is your office, whether you've actually placed a desk here or you use your dining table as your desk, you can still support your wealth. An elegant looking pair of candlesticks, a decorative dish on the buffet or the center of your table, or a crystal dish on your desk that holds your paper clips can be your wealth tools.

Surround yourself with things that make you feel wealthy. Would The Donald use a paper cup to hold his paper clips? Again, the things you use don't have to *be* expensive, they just need to *look* expensive or give you the *feel* of wealth. They should make you feel good about your space, even spoiled. They should not make you feel depressed or poor.

If your dining room is now a playroom, the tricky part of this is clutter: wealth doesn't like clutter, and playrooms tend to be all about clutter. Active clutter, things in progress, such as a partially built castle of blocks, is fine. It's the toys and games that are left strewn about and forgotten that can drain valuable Chi – life energy – and wealth.

To avoid draining Chi, ensure there is sufficient storage for the toys. Whether that means book shelves or storage bins or baskets, or even curtains or partitions to hide the bigger items, these tools can help keep the energy clear and flowing. Clutter tends to trap, and thus can stagnate, the energy, which can drain wealth, not to mention drain your mood or productivity.

As with the playroom, if your dining room has become a storage space, keep it neat and organized. Use the buffet or hutch to hold those old magazines that you can't part with. Storage can be added in ways that will blend with the room and change those piles into strength and support. An armoire, while adding valuable storage space, can add a sense of stability, which is a good thing to associate with wealth.

And if, by chance, your dining room is still a dining room, you've got it easy. A table runner or a tablecloth can wealth-up the table. Placemats can do this also, as well as candlesticks, a centerpiece, chair covers and more. Accessories, in general, will increase the wealth vibe of the dining room. Choose them carefully and they will work doubly well for you.

Does your dining room remind you of a mansion or a royal palace? Then you are on the right track. Does it remind you of a cabin in the woods or an all-you-can-eat buffet? Then it's probably not helping your wealth situation.

If you use this area frequently, then make sure you experience the "royal treatment" in this room. If you use it only a few times a year for holidays or other occasions, it should make a royal statement when you walk past it, even though you don't spend time in it.

See Exercise #11 on the following page.

Exercise #11

Guess Who's Coming to Dinner?

If the Queen were coming to dinner at your home this evening, would you have a place to dine that would not cause you embarrassment? If it's another area, such as an eat-in kitchen, that is fine, too. What would you have to do to really make it ready for her (or whichever public figure you admire), or for your future in-laws?

Step 1. If important guests were coming to dinner at your home this evening, what would you want or need to do before they arrived? Make a list of the things you would do to make your dining room ready for them.

Step 2. Suppose you don't have time to finish them all. Rank them in order of importance.

Step 3. Are there any items on the list that you could easily complete in the next few days or weeks? Do them…and you will be starting the shift in Chi that affects your wealth.

Your Bathroom

The bathroom is the last of what I consider the "public" rooms. It is a room that is often misunderstood when it comes to Feng Shui. For example, some say:

- A bathroom is naturally bad Feng Shui.

- Keep the door shut.

- Keep the toilet lid down.

- Keep your drains closed.

- It shouldn't be in the center of the home.

- Place a mirror under the toilet.

These are some of the more common comments I hear about Feng Shui and bathrooms. I'll address each of them; but first, a bit of history.

When Feng Shui was developed several thousand years ago, there was no indoor plumbing. There were no bathrooms. Bathrooms, were bushes outdoors. Many years later, indoor closets were built, with a hole in the ground for the toilet. These were not good Feng Shui. Then indoor plumbing arrived, but only the wealthy had the means to install it.

Are you following this? In my opinion, bathrooms went from being outdoors and unrelated to the Feng Shui of the home, to being indoors and being bad Feng Shui, to being indoors for the wealthy. *The wealthy!* So when did it turn back to being bad Feng Shui rather than being something associated with wealth? The answer is probably in the misunderstanding of bathroom Feng Shui that is so prevalent.

Now let's take a look at each myth listed above.

A bathroom is naturally bad Feng Shui. When you see a lovely bathroom, how can you see that as being bad Feng Shui? I just don't see bathrooms as being automatically bad Feng Shui. Now, if it is a dirty, grimy, cluttered mess, then it would stand to reason that it is bad Feng Shui. But that is not by nature of simply being a bathroom; it is by nature of the care it is given.

Keep the door shut. Keeping the door shut is not a rule that must always be followed. Each home is different. Is the bathroom visible from the kitchen or dining room? Then you probably want to close the door so your guests aren't looking at the toilet while they eat.

Is the bathroom visible from your bed? If so, then close the door (unless you consider a toilet romantic).

Are you following this logic? If the room is not prominent, then closing the door may not be necessary. A point that needs addressing is the Feng Shui energy chart of your home. If the bathroom is in an area of the home that is not favorable energy, then closing the door can help from spreading that energy around the home.

However, if it is located in an area with favorable energy, closing the door could block that energy from being shared with the entire home. If you don't know the energetic chart of your home, you'll need to trust your instincts or invest in having a Feng Shui professional calculate your chart for you.

Keep the toilet lid down. This statement has several points to consider. Do you have children or pets who could get into the toilet? Is the toilet visible from another area of the home? How about for health reasons? Closing the lid before flushing will prevent the germs from being sprayed about the room.

Keep your drains closed. It has been said that keeping the drains closed will prevent valuable Chi from escaping down your drain, and your wealth along with it. In an airplane, which is pressurized, this may in fact be true. But in a home? I will leave that up to you. I suggest trying it both ways and see which feels best to you. If you are feeling your wealth is being drained, consider closing the drains. However, if you are feeling things are stagnant, opening the drains may in fact create movement.

It's bad Feng Shui to have a bathroom in the center of the home. To me, it depends upon what the energy is at the center of the home. If you have a favorable energy in the center of your home and your bathroom is located there, then it's likely the favorable energy will be "trapped" in this small room.

If you are shopping for a new home, would a bathroom in the center of the home be a deal-breaker? That, in and of itself, is not a deal-breaker for me. I would need to determine the energetic chart of the home. It would also depend upon the condition of the bathroom and the movement to and from it.

Place a mirror under the toilet. Well, not exactly. The practice is to place a mirror *in front* of the toilet. The mirror should be the length and the width of the toilet and should be facing the toilet. But who wants this??? Not most people! And, not every toilet needs a mirror. It depends upon what is on the other side of the toilet.

Negative energy, Sheng Chi, comes out from the toilet. Over time, this can create health issues. These issues will be addressed in more detail in the next book in this series, which concentrates on health. For now, know that placing a mirror under or behind your toilet is not doing much of anything for your wealth from a Feng Shui perspective.

Of course, I have to address clutter in the bathroom. Who doesn't have clutter here? We use this room for short periods of time, often while rushing to get ready to leave the house. Most of us do not take the time or effort to put things away that we will just take out again the next time we are rushing to leave.

Does it look wealthy to you when you walk into your bathroom and your grooming products are strewn all over the counter? Can you put some of them away and leave some of them out? Are the caps or covers on the bottles and tubes? Find your personal balance between functionality and inspiring wealth.

By now you are likely beginning to see a couple of patterns emerging:

1. Clutter is not good for wealth.
2. Feng Shui is not black and white; there are many factors that determine whether something is favorable or not.

Exercise #12

Is Your Throne Fit for a Queen?

What would it take for your bathroom to be royalty-ready? Here's a simple check list you can follow to get started:

- Clear clutter off countertops.

- Towels are neatly hung, and guest towels are available.

- It is a soothing place for relaxing in a tub/shower rather than a hurried place of getting ready for work.

- Personal (and feminine) hygiene products are out of sight.

- Palace versus gas station: which does your bathroom remind you of?

Optional:

- Is the toilet lid down?

- Is the door closed?

Your Closet

The often dreaded and avoided "storage" closet; is there room in yours to receive? You may think a closet stuffed full of clothes indicates wealth, but it could actually be blocking you from receiving further. Do you wear everything that is currently hanging in your closet? Do you have clothes that don't fit or are out of style?

Perhaps you have clothes that are worn or stained but for some reason you can't seem to part with them. Why is that? Are you afraid you won't be able to replace them? That fear is actually an indicator of scarcity. Scarcity is the opposite of wealth. Can you understand that keeping these things may be going against your desire for wealth?

If you have clothes for certain occasions, such as evening gowns or holiday sweaters, can they be stored someplace else to leave breathing space in your closet? Remember that being organized allows you to store more things in the same amount of space.

Why are you keeping things that are old or worn or do not fit you? Are you hoping to wear them again one day? If they are a bit snug and, thus, slightly uncomfortable, keep them. But if they are a few sizes too small, why are you keeping them? Do you think that when you shrink a few sizes you won't have the money to buy new clothes that fit you?

Do you have a favorite or beloved dress or outfit that doesn't fit? Fine, keep one or two of those; but is it really necessary to keep the entire wardrobe?

If your closet is so full that you can't find what you need, then it's time to do some clearing. Or perhaps your closet is so disorganized that you can't find what you want when you need it. This may be true for bedroom closets, hall closets, pantries, etc. All closets need space, or breathing room.

> **Exercise #13**
>
> Abundance or scarcity: What does your closet say?
>
> Can you easily find a particular item of clothing you want to wear? Do you have clothes that you haven't worn in years? Do you have room for the perfect black dress you may find next week when you go shopping with a friend or for that amazing pair of shoes you see while you are strolling at lunch time?
>
> Make room for new things. Release things that no longer serve you. The Clutter Guide included at the end of the book is a great tool for cleaning out closets and making them wealth-ready.
>
> Consider asking a friend to help you. She won't have an emotional attachment to your clothes and will be able to offer an objective opinion on whether or not they are closet-worthy.

We've looked at the various rooms and locations inside your home; now let's look at the accessories you've chosen with which to surround yourself.

Your Art

It's important that the art on your walls reflects what you want to attract into your life. Think of the walls of your home as a *Life-sized, 3-D Vision Board*™. Choose what you include in your vision board carefully.

If you've been paying attention to all the talk these days about how powerful our thoughts are in determining what our lives look like, then you'll understand what I'm talking about. What we see generates thoughts and images in our brain, just like what we hear or think. Be clear on what you want to draw into your life, and make sure the art in your environment reflects that.

Art doesn't have to depict just one thing. For example, if what you want is to travel and be in a loving relationship, then look for art that depicts a couple in love in locations you would like to visit, such as a couple kissing with the Eiffel Tower in the background.

If what you want is a large home in the mountains, then find a lithograph of this. Do you want to own the home or rent it for a vacation? If you want to own it, consider finding similar photos depicting different seasons. If you just want a time-share in the mountains during ski season, then you will only need a photo of a grand home surrounded by snow.

There may be some pieces of art in your home that will be neutral. That's okay. Don't get too obsessive about making every piece of art or every piece of furniture in your environment perfect for your vision board or your dream home. There will be neutrals – things that have no emotional reaction from you – and many of these may have a functional purpose. Those are fine to have around.

The most important step is to remove the things that definitely are not in alignment with your goals, dreams, visions or desires. Those things could be holding you back from reaching your goals.

If those things reflect who you were in the past, make sure they don't outnumber the items that reflect where you are headed, or you could find yourself stuck in the past.

Of course, some things from your past are very important to have around. They can keep you grounded in your roots, keeping you close to family and friends or to mentors and teachers who have been important to your growth.

Remember that wealth is not just about acquiring physical objects, so be sure you are clear about how life would be different for you. How would you feel if you were wealthy? What types of things would you do? Where would you go? With whom would you spend your time? Make sure the art you display reflects these visions.

As you create your life-sized vision board on your walls, be advised that things may need to be changed again. Feng Shui, unlike interior decorating, will evolve as you and your life evolve.

What is representative of a vision of yours now may not be in a few weeks or months or years. As you set up your life-sized, 3-D vision board™, things in your life will shift. You will notice that you have achieved some of your goals. You will then set new goals. You'll want to update your art to reflect your new goals—or you will be reinforcing your current status but not accessing opportunities to grow.

Exercise #14

Take an inventory of the art currently hanging on your walls. Walk through your home and look at each item on your walls. Since we are discussing wealth, create two columns on a piece of paper. Label one "Princess" and the other "Pauper."

As you walk through your home and look at each piece of art, put a tic mark under the appropriate column for each item. If a picture doesn't clearly depict Princess, or you have to stop and think about whether it does or not, then it is a Pauper.

This may seem rigid to you but, remember, we are looking to see how many items represent your goals. You want them to be clear and obvious. If an item doesn't clearly show wealth, then you likely wouldn't cut that picture out of a magazine to include it in a vision board. If that is the case, then you may not want it on your life-sized, 3-D vision board.

If you have other interests or goals, such as a relationship, travel, or a hobby, you also may want to note if each item represents and supports any of these goals or not.

Continued on the following page.

Exercise #14 Continued

Remember, one item can represent several goals. For example, a picture of a couple on a sandy beach with a yacht in the background could represent a relationship, travel and wealth.

It's okay to have some neutral items; the important thing is to be sure you have enough items representing your wealth goals to be supportive. Taking the inventory looking strictly between Princess and Pauper will help.

Your Furniture
&
Home Accessories

Let's do something different and start this chapter with an exercise.an exercise.

> **Exercise #15 – Part I**
>
> Look at your furniture. Describe it with one word. Don't think about it; go with the first word that comes to mind. Is it casual? Comfortable? Elegant? Dirty? Old? Worn? Ugly? Girly? Boring? Pretty? Soothing? Quirky?
>
> After identifying the one-word description, think about what that word means to you. Does it give you a positive feeling or a negative feeling? Does it make you happy? Sad? Angry? Energized? Inspired? Depressed? Do you judge it? Do you feel like you need to justify or explain it?
>
> Do you relate to that word? How? Would you use that same word to describe yourself? Perhaps it describes you in the past, or maybe it describes who you want to be in the future?

What do you now know about your furniture that you did not know before? Perhaps you already knew your furniture was old, dirty or depressing. Had you been ignoring that? If so, that was draining you of valuable Chi – life energy.

The energy you spend denying how you feel about your furniture could be used toward reaching your wealth goals.

Which would you rather spend your energy on: your goals or denial?

Furniture can be a costly investment. Maybe you can get by with empty walls for a while but you likely can't go without furniture until you can afford your dream sofa.

So what can you do? Just like jewelry can change the look and feel of an outfit by dressing it up or down, accessories can change the look and feel of a room. Pillows, slip covers, or throws can help change the look and feel of your furniture and your room. If you want your room to look wealthy, choose a few ornate pillows. Gold trim, brocade patterns, or a lush velvety texture will bring a statement of wealth.

Cleaning the upholstery yourself or having it professionally cleaned can also make a big difference. Rearranging the furniture is another great option that can help re-energize how a room looks without getting new furniture. It will also give you a new perspective if you sit in the same old chair but are facing a different direction.

Consider replacing one piece. You can do this by swapping out one item in a room with an item from another room. A simple swap like this can lift the energy. It may help you see other simple ways to lift the energy. It may lead to a rearrangement of the other objects that you may not have considered otherwise. It could transform a room you don't like into a room that feels cozy and inviting.

Whenever possible, make sure you have at least one piece of furniture that you truly love, and would take with you to your dream home, in each room. Avoid having a room that is entirely the left-over pieces that don't belong anywhere else, or all the pieces that you don't like. This could lead to a useful room being a room you avoid. If you can spare a room, that may be fine. But make sure that the view as you walk past this room isn't draining or depressing.

If you have one great piece in a room, one that pops, your guests are a lot less likely to notice the not-so-new sofa. They'll be far too distracted by the beautiful or unique piece that catches their attention to notice the drab sofa, regardless of where they are sitting.

Try splitting up a set. Consider breaking up your beloved living room set by moving one of the pieces into that spare room that you never spend time in. That chair may be just what you need in your bedroom or guest room. Maybe one of the dressers in your bedroom can go into the hallway or kitchen for your table linens.

Just one piece can make a huge difference in how a room feels. One beloved piece of furniture along with one beloved piece of art can miraculously turn a room from dingy to dynamic.

Exercise #15 – Part II

Think again about the word you used to describe your furniture. What word would you like to be able to use to describe it? Is there a piece of furniture in your home that fits that word? Would moving that piece from one room to another change the description?

Include one piece of furniture in each room that you would definitely bring into your dream home. If possible, have a piece that "screams" wealth to you. Whether or not it costs a lot of money, does it look wealthy or somehow represent wealth to you? If so, then it is a piece that should be in an area where you spend a lot of time, or placed in a room so that it is visible as you walk past that room. Place it near a door to act as your "greeter" so you and your guests are welcomed home by something that makes a statement of wealth.

So far, we've spent a lot of time inside your home. Now let's take a quick look at the things and places outside your home that can impact your wealth.

The Palace Grounds

Now that you've reviewed your inside space, it's time to look at your outside space. Most anyone would be surprised to see a neat and elegant home inside that has an overgrown, unkempt yard outside. But it does happen.

Whether you own a home on several acres of land or rent a studio apartment, you can tend to the path to your grounds. You may have a patio or a small balcony, or perhaps just windows that are visible from the street or sidewalk.

Let me take this opportunity to also address the garage. You may have a garage and, whether attached or not, it is part of your space. Balancing the energy of a garage using traditional (compass) methods of Feng Shui will depend upon the location of the garage, how you use it, and its accessibility to the home.

Yet, your garage is part of your space and does impact your wealth consciousness. Is it neat and organized? Do you use it to store your car, as it is intended, or do you use it for the extra furniture or boxes? Do you use it as a work space, or have you converted it to a gym or a game room?

If it's been converted to some purpose other than storage for cars or other objects, refer to the most fitting chapter and apply the techniques therein. For those who store their cars or other objects in the garage, is it organized? Can you find what you need when you need it without risk of life or limb?

If this is how you generally enter and leave your home, is it inviting? Does it represent wealth or are you using the "servant's entrance" to the palace? If your garage doesn't house the car of your dreams, consider hanging a poster of the car of your dreams, framed for wealth, in your garage.

Exercise #16

People often judge and assess based on appearance. Take a stroll through your grounds. Observe what pleases you and what displeases you. Make a list of what needs to be tended to. Also make note of the areas in which you want to linger and why. Does it invite lingering by way of a bench, a chair, a large flat-topped rock, or a hammock?

Can you create that same feeling elsewhere? How much effort would that take? Is that an effort you are willing to put forth? You may not need to create another space like this within your yard. Perhaps you can create one or more spaces in your yard that have a *view* of this location. A view of a space is the next best thing to being there.

You can start simple by sweeping, adding a few more plants, clearing dead leaves, painting the rusted table, replacing worn seat cushions for the chairs, or adding a statue or a light post.

To create a place that is relaxing and pleasant, the first step is often to remove clutter: tools, wood remnants, empty pots or planter boxes, or a rusted bike that you never use.

Exercise #16 (Continued)

Clutter drains wealth. Yards and garages are often magnets for clutter. If you were wealthy, by your description, which of the things in your yard and garage would you release? Do you need these things to acquire your wealth, or are you keeping them out of fear of scarcity?

Scarcity breeds scarcity, not wealth. Release at least 3 items from your yard and/or garage.

Your Car

In dream interpretation, a car represents the body. This could apply loosely to Feng Shui as well. The car you drive is a reflection of you. Not just the make or model, but how you care for it. Do you treat it with respect, inside and out?

People are often judged by the kind of car they drive. But it goes beyond that. How a person treats their belongings is often an indication of how they treat themselves. It is rare to find a person who is impeccably dressed and well groomed but drives a car that is running rough, is in need of a wash, or perhaps even needs some body work.

Just because you may not have the means to treat yourself to the car of your dreams doesn't mean you have to look like a pauper when you drive down the road. Taking pride in your presentation, by means of car care, is an important step in attracting wealth.

Remember in the story of Cinderella how she had to leave the ball by the stroke of midnight to make sure her carriage didn't turn into a pumpkin? Presentation is very important. Perhaps car presentation is more important in Los Angeles than in some other cities, but regardless of where you live, pride in the care of your vehicle is important.

Just like in a job, where you must succeed at certain tasks before you are given more responsibility or more important tasks, in the pursuit of wealth one must succeed at their current level of wealth before going on to the next level. Whatever level you are at, succeed at it.

Have you ever seen a dirty or dented limo or Jaguar? If so, it was likely on its way to the car wash or the body shop. Do those cars smell like fast food or garbage inside? Not likely. So if you want to *have* wealth, *act* as if you already have it.

Treat your vehicle with pride, no matter what kind of car you drive. Be grateful for your car, for how it delivers you safely from place to place. Appreciate it and be proud of it. Gratitude is the key.

One tenet of Feng Shui is that everything is alive. To make this easier to comprehend, imagine that your car is a person. What do you say to the person that is your car? Do you criticize it or call it names? Do you hit it or kick it? Do you keep it well fed with fuel or do you practically starve it before feeding it again? Do you feed it a full tank of gas or just a snack here and there? Do you bathe it and take it to the doctor? Do you treat injuries or let them get infected?

If your car were a person that you treated this way, how would it treat you in return? Would it honor you with gifts, money, rewards, and appreciation? Or would it turn its back on you and dismiss you—or perhaps try to sabotage you?

Exercise #17

Is your car a pumpkin or a royal carriage? If you had your dream car, how would you treat it? How does that compare to how you treat your current car?

Would you park it in the same place?

Would you wash/wax it with the same frequency?

Would you keep the same items in the back seat, the passenger seat, or the trunk?

Would you eat in it like you do now?

Pick one or more items that you feel comfortable working on, and begin to change how you treat your current car. Treat your car like your dream car, and your dream car may just show up.

Your Place of Work

If you were around during the 1980s you may recall the surge of the "yuppie" (young urban professionals) movement and how most were working long hours. I know I had friends who thought it was impressive when they told people they were working 10-12 hour days. In their minds, it gave them prestige.

What is your opinion of this? Would you work long days if you had wealth? I'm not suggesting that you don't put in the effort that is needed to maintain your work and increase your wealth. There are very few people who don't work hard to earn and/or maintain their wealth.

Do you like what you do? Do you respect what you do? Do you appreciate the job you have? For many people, their job is how they earn their income, or at least the majority of it. It's how we build our wealth. Pay attention to it. Pay attention to how you speak about it, how you think about it, and how you feel about it.

Sure, if money weren't an issue you may be doing something completely different, but can you appreciate your work for what it does provide? Appreciating what we have can lead to receiving more or better things into our lives.

Do you honor your place of work by being mindful of your workspace? Is it clean and clutter-free? Remember there is a difference between active and stagnant clutter; review that chapter if needed or use the clutter clearing guide.

See Exercise #18 on the following page.

Exercise #18

Take an inventory of personal items in your work space. Are they photos of loved ones? Are they toys or games? Are they success oriented? Do they distract you from work?

Would they call attention from a visiting executive? Is that good attention or not?

If someone were to select you for a promotion based strictly on how your work space looks, would you get the position? Would you hire yourself based on the look and feel of your work space?

What changes do you see that you can make to improve your promotability?

Your Purse & Wallet

Respect is the keyword in this chapter. Treat your purse and/or wallet with respect and it, as well as your money, will show you respect. For hundreds or maybe even thousands of years men have concerned themselves with money—how to earn it and how to spend it. This is a relatively new commodity for women. Learn from men.

When was the last time you went out to dinner with a man and he pulled out his wallet and set it on the floor? *Never.* So why do so many women put their wallet, albeit inside their purse, on the floor? Avoid doing this whenever possible. I realize there may be some occasions when you can't avoid it, but the point is to be mindful of doing it or, rather, mindful of *not* doing it whenever possible.

Would you throw your money on the floor? Then just because it is inside a wallet, purse or bag, it still doesn't belong on the floor. Haphazardly tossing something on the floor is disrespectful. Treat your money, and the accessory you keep it in, with respect.

Do you stuff your money in a pocket of your pants or your purse, rather than a wallet or some other item designed to hold money? Again, remember, this is not a "rule" that shouldn't ever be broken. This is about gaining an understanding of the energy or vibe you are creating and being mindful of it.

If you are going out to a nightclub or a sporting activity and carrying a purse or wallet doesn't make sense, it's perfectly fine to consciously choose to put your money in a pocket…with care and respect. Do you see that this is treating your money with respect? It is quite different than just shoving a wad of bills into a pocket because you have no place else to put them.

What do you use to carry your money? Do you use a paper clip as a "money clip"? Do you use a rubber band or a hair band of some kind? It's fine to use whatever system works best for you. However, use something that is respectful and representative of wealth.

For example, a used rubber band that came off the daily newspaper isn't respectful. If you buy an attractive hair band specifically for holding your money, that is respectful. Rule of thumb: Leftover = not respectful; intentional = respectful.

Do you use a wallet or a change purse? Select one that you are proud for others to see. It doesn't have to be expensive, but it can be. It may be something you choose to invest in so that each time you open it you are reminded of the wealth you had to buy the wallet.

And it doesn't have to be expensive, as long as it makes you feel good and feel proud to see it and have it be seen. If the money holder is too worn or outdated, you may want to consider investing in another means of carrying your money. If you use something that has sentimental value, be sure that it doesn't have an association with a person or a time in your life when you or they didn't have money. Unless, of course, seeing it brings a smile to your face and causes you to acknowledge the road you traveled and the success you've achieved.

So what would be an appropriate means to carry your money? Just about anything. Even an envelope if that is what you choose to use, as long as it's not an envelope that a bill came in. It can be a plain white envelope or, better yet, an attractive envelope from a stationary store.

It's traditional, in China, to give money in small red envelopes. Something like this would be a perfect envelope to use; however, they don't hold much. You could do what I do, which is carry my credit cards and store discount cards in one of these red envelopes. They usually have a gold inscription of some kind. If you buy them online or in a Chinese market, they will have them labeled or the clerk should be able to tell you which one is for prosperity. Some may be for specific events such as weddings or the birth of a child, so be sure that you are selecting a prosperity envelope.

Exercise #19

When was the last time you went through your purse; I mean, *really* went through your purse? Let's do it together.

1. Empty the entire contents.

2. Clean the inside of your purse. Remove the clumps of lint wedged in the seams of the lining. Clean the outside, too.

3. Did you notice if any repairs are needed? If so, find an alternate purse to use so you can get the repairs done as soon as possible. Or perhaps your purse needs to be replaced altogether. You decide, but whatever the case, do *not* put the contents back into a purse that needs repair or replacement.

Continued on the following page.

Exercise #19 Continued

4. Go through the contents and sort items into 3 piles:

    What you use often

    What you use infrequently but want to carry with you

    What you do not need to carry

5. Go through steps 1-4 with your wallet.

6. Return items to your wallet that you use often. Do this in an organized way, making them easily accessible.

7. If you have room for more items in your wallet, add in some or all of the things you use infrequently but would like to carry. If there is no more room in your wallet, consider adding another item such as a "make-up" bag that you can use to store these items, allowing them to be easily added or removed as needed.

8. Throw away trash and find a home for the things you do not need to carry.

Exercise #19 Continued

9. Go through steps 6 – 8 for returning the contents to your purse.

10. Your purse should now have room to acquire more wealth. It should make you feel good to carry it and be easy to search through the contents for whatever it is you need. Remember, wealth does not like clutter; so remove clutter from your purse and wallet and make room for wealth.

Appendix A:
Clutter Clearing Guide

II

3 Easy Steps To Clear Your Clutter

Are you ready to clear the clutter out of your home or office?

Follow these three easy steps and you'll be amazed at how much more peaceful and energized you feel. Of course, your space will look great, too!

Step 1

Sort each item into one of the following three categories:

1. Things I love and definitely want to keep.
2. Things I definitely will clear out of my space.
3. Things I am not sure about.

Don't let the items you are unsure about slow down your momentum. Toss them in the third pile and keep going. It is often the "unsure" items that cause people to get discouraged, lose motivation, and give up on their clutter clearing. When you are done, you can go back through the unsure pile and sort again. You'll be amazed that when you go through it a second time, you'll find many things you are now sure you want to get rid of. And don't forget to have that third pile available when you go through it a second time.

Step 2

Now that you have a number of things you know you want to get rid of, identify the options you have for disposing of those things. Some people are stopped here: they've identified what they want to release but don't know how or where so they end up keeping the items. Don't let that happen to you! Here are several options to consider:

- <u>Sell it</u> – Be sure you are willing to go through the effort to sell it *now*, not months from now. Have a garage sale, sell it on eBay, place an ad in a local paper, or post it on Craig's List.

- <u>Give it to someone</u> – If you know someone who would love it, then go ahead and give it to them. They'll be thrilled to get an unexpected gift from you.

- <u>Lend it</u> – This is great for those things you don't want to give up forever but don't need or have room for right now. Loan it to someone who could use it. But if you don't already know someone who could use it, be careful that you don't end up keeping it under the guise of finding someone to lend it to later. If finding the right borrower takes more time or effort than you are willing to spend, then consider the next option.

- <u>Donate it</u> – If it's in good condition, find a local charitable organization to donate it to. Schools, churches, clubs and other organizations are viable options along with Good Will, Salvation Army, the American Cancer Society, and other well-known groups.

- <u>Recycle it</u> – Is it made of plastic, glass, aluminum, paper, or other recyclable materials? Is it a computer? Does it have batteries in it? If so, do the environment a favor and recycle it. Did you know that California law requires all stores that sell batteries to recycle them? So don't toss your batteries in the trash; take them back to CVS, Target, Vons, or wherever you may have purchased them.

And finally:

- <u>Throw it away</u> – Is it outdated, worn, or broken and not repairable? I use this option as a last resort so that my unwanted clutter doesn't clutter the environment. But sometimes this is the only option, so allow yourself to use this when needed to keep your home clear.

Step 3

To really clear out all unnecessary clutter, make sure you are keeping only those things that are really necessary or loved. Below is a list of questions you can ask yourself about *each and every* item in your space.

- Do you **love it** now? This is different than "did you once love it?" If you no longer love it, maybe it doesn't belong in your space.

- Do you **need it/use it** regularly? The word "regularly" is subjective. Is it a seasonal or holiday item that you use year after year? If so, keep it. If it's something you keep for "when I might need it," perhaps it's time to let it go.

- Does it **represent** who you are in your life now...or who you were in your past? If it represents your past, you may want to release it and keep your past *in your past,* not in your environment.

- Does it **support** you and your goals by being in your space? If so, great; if not, why are you holding on to it?

- When you look at it, do you get positive, happy thoughts, feelings or memories? Does it give you mixed feelings? Decide if it is more positive or not, and that will guide you whether to keep it or not.

- Does it need to be repaired and are you willing to do so? If not, then there is no reason to keep it.

- Would you take it with you if you were moving into your new dream home today?

- Does it represent what you are intending to manifest in your life?

Congratulations! Now you are armed with the skills you need to begin successfully clearing your clutter. Don't wait—get started today to experience the energy of a cleaner space. Clear out three items today to get the flow started.

Think of your home or office as an over-weighted boat that's skimming just above the water surface; the sooner you lose heavy cargo, the sooner the boat will rise up and move forward with ease on your journey.

GOOD LUCK AND ENJOY YOUR NEWLY CLEARED SPACE WITH ROOM TO RECEIVE!

Appendix B:

Recommended Reading

Recommended Reading

Move Your Stuff, Change Your Life
Karen Rauch Carter

The Western Guide to Feng Shui for Prosperity
Terah Kathryn Collins

The Complete Idiot's Guide to Feng Shui
Elizabeth Moran, Master Joseph Yu,
and Master Val Biktashev

Clear Your Clutter with FENG SHUI
Karen Kingston

Who Moved My Cheese?
Spencer Johnson, M.D.

The Four Agreements
Don Miguel Ruiz

The Alchemist
Paulo Coelho

The Knight in Rusty Armor
Robert Fisher

Three Feet from Gold
Sharon L. Lechter & Greg S. Reid

Think and Grow Rich
Napoleon Hill

XIV

Coming Soon!

Athlete or Ailing

Is Your Home's Feng Shui Affecting Your Health?

The third in the series

Walls *Do* Talk

By

Helen Arabanos

About the Author

Helen Arabanos was born and raised in Minneapolis and graduated from the University of Minnesota with a B.A. in Statistics. She started her career in the field of Market Research Analysis and moved into the field of Technology, with an emphasis in Call Center Management and Data Analysis.

How does someone with a background in statistics and technology become a Feng Shui Expert? Helen became fascinated when she realized how practical Feng Shui is. Surprisingly, many of the same skills are used. Skills that make her such a qualified Feng Shui Practitioner include: data gathering, data analyzing, and making recommendations based on the analysis of data.

In the mid-1980's Helen was introduced to Feng Shui by a man from China at a chance lunch-time encounter. From there she began her quest for more information on this ancient subject. Yet she remembers when she was a child, maybe 8 years old, she used to draw floor plans, cut out furniture shapes, and place them around the floor plan based on how she felt. She placed them at angles and felt that certain colors were needed in each area. At the time, she wasn't aware that she was tuning into the energy and what was needed to create balance.

Helen is a graduate of the Western School of Feng Shui in San Diego, California and has studied with many Masters from around the world. She is trained in both Western style Feng Shui and the traditional Feng Shui methods of Flying Star and 8 Mansions. Helen has studied other modalities including Reiki Healing, Chinese Face Reading, Four

Pillars Astrology, and Dowsing. She is also a skilled and accurate Tarot Reader.

For almost a decade, Helen has helped people from all walks of life including celebrities, students, business owners, and people working in a variety of industries. Her business, Full Bloom Feng Shui, was established in 2005, at which time she left the corporate world to run her Feng Shui business. Her corporate experience is invaluable when she is consulting with her corporate clients.

Helen currently resides in the Los Angeles area.

For more information about Helen or to inquire about her Feng Shui Consulting services, visit her website: www.FullBloomFengShui.com *We Heal Homes*

FREE
Wealth Tips

Visit

www.FullBloomFengShui.com/princess

It's like having your own wealth coach guiding you along your way to wealth, prosperity and abundance!

www.ingramcontent.com/pod-product-compliance
Lightning Source LLC
Chambersburg PA
CBHW071013200526
45171CB00007B/82